ENERGY BITES

First published in Great Britain in 2018 by Modern Books
An imprint of Elwin Street Productions Limited
14 Clerkenwell Green
London EC1R 0DP
www.modern-books.com

ISBN: 978-1-911130-15-4

10 9 8 7 6 5 4 3 2 1

Picture Credits:
Photographs by Uyen Luu, except Alamy Stock Photo: p 24;
Shutterstock: pp 21, 25.

Printed in China

ENERGY BITES

CHRISTINE BAILEY

HIGH-PROTEIN, NO-BAKE BLISS BALLS TO MAKE AND GIVE

CONTENTS

BITES WITH BENEFITS

When made with nutritious ingredients, energy bites are pretty much the perfect snack. They have a great combination of protein, carbohydrates and healthy fats. When you make your own you can customize them to your taste and requirements and save yourself money on store-bought bars and bites – many of which are loaded with sugars and additives.

What's unique about this book is that all the recipes focus on keeping the sugar and fructose content low, and all use nutritious ingredients – no cooking required! Unlike most pre-packaged bites or recipes on the internet, these do not rely on syrups, dates or excess fruits but rather use a range of delicious natural ingredients to provide sweetness without upsetting your blood sugar levels. Many of the bites are good sources of protein and fibre, too, which helps to keep you feeling fuller for longer, avoiding energy dips which can lead to hunger pangs and cravings. This makes them ideal for pre- and post-workout snacks, grab-and-go breakfast options as well as packed lunch treats and afternoon work snacks. We have also included a number of more indulgent recipes, perfect for special occasions, gifts or healthy treats.

If you're following a special diet you will also find recipes to suit you. All of the recipes can be made gluten free and many are suitable for raw, paleo and vegan diets too. We've included notes and helpful tips for tweaking recipes and substituting ingredients to meet your preferences.

The chapters have been organized to help you choose the best recipes for your needs. Fitness Boosters will help you get the most out of your exercise whether you are a seasoned gym-goer, keen athlete or just like to keep active and healthy. Many of the bites include specific ingredients known to help boost performance, recovery and repair, as well as support healthy muscle mass or promote fat loss.

On the Run contains a fabulous selection of bites for everyday eating – whether it's a breakfast on the go, packed lunches or something to boost energy levels after the daily chores. These recipes are made with familiar ingredients to enable you to whizz up a batch with ease.

Fancy something more indulgent and sweetly satisfying? Then take a look at Gifts and Indulgences. They are ideal gifts you can make for family and friends.

ONE

GETTING STARTED

Here is all you need to know before getting stuck in to the recipes. Find out why the bites in this book are healthier than any others you can buy, and stock up on all the essential ingredients you'll need for making your own delicious energy bites at home. There's even a guide to making your own nut butter.

WHAT YOU NEED

Free from preservatives and packed with protein, fibre and good fats, energy bites are easy to make at home, with little cooking required. You're now en route to making delicious energy bites that are healthy for you and tasty to boot – the hardest part is choosing which recipe to start with!

In this section of the book you will find information on the essential ingredients that form the building blocks of energy bites, and the benefits of each one. After you've tried out the yummy combinations suggested in this book, you can even start customizing the recipes to your personal taste.

NUTRITIONAL VALUES

All the recipes in this book have been created to give both optimum nutritional value as well as maximum taste, and a nutritional breakdown is listed for each one. Be aware that the recipes have been created with low sugar content in mind, so if you do make substitutions, particularly by adding fruit or sweeteners, these health benefits will change. For more information on natural ways to sweeten, see page 19.

A WORD ON EQUIPMENT

Energy bites are simple to create using everyday kitchen tools, but you may find a few items handy to make the job quicker.

A food processor or blender is the easiest tool to use for whipping up the energy bites. You can chop up the ingredients finely by hand, but this can be a time-consuming process.

Baking trays are useful for placing the balls after shaping, and chilling in the fridge or freezer.

Dehydrators allow you to make your own "activated" nuts for a nut butter that is easy to digest, but still delivers on flavour. It certainly isn't an essential tool for making energy bites, but a homemade activated nut butter is a fun upgrade for recipes (see page 22).

RAW MATERIALS

DRY INGREDIENTS

Nuts are incredibly nutrient-dense with a good combination of healthy fats and protein. They can also supply essential vitamins and minerals including zinc, calcium, B vitamins, magnesium, potassium and manganese.

In many of the recipes the types of nuts are interchangeable. You can grind them to form a flour as the base of bites or you can use them finely chopped to add texture.

Seeds are equally nutrient-dense and some such as chia, flaxseed and hemp are also rich in the essential omega-3 fatty acids which are important for heart health, lowering inflammation and supporting brain function. Ground seeds are readily available or you can grind your own in a blender, juicer or food processor.

Ground flaxseed and chia seeds are very absorbent and can be used interchangeably with each other but not as a replacement for other seeds or nuts. They are particularly useful to help bind the energy bites.

Desiccated coconut and coconut flakes (choose unsweetened brands) are simply coconut flesh that has been grated and dried. They are a good source of fibre, manganese and copper which supports energy production. They also contain medium-chain triglycerides – a type of saturated fat the body can use readily for energy.

Porridge oats and gluten-free grains provide a nutritious base in energy bites. Oats are high in fibre, including beta glucans, which have been shown to support immune health and lower cholesterol. With their low glycaemic index (GI), oats help balance blood sugar levels, keeping you energized and feeling fuller for longer. Oats are also packed with an array of vitamins and minerals including B vitamins, magnesium, zinc and manganese.

If you are following a gluten-free diet, make sure you select certified gluten-free oats or use an alternative such as quinoa, millet, buckwheat flakes or puffed rice.

Coconut flour is a popular gluten-free and paleo-friendly flour, commonly used in baking and recipes. Made from ground and dried coconut flesh, it is low in carbohydrates, high in fibre and a good source of energizing medium-chain fatty acids. It is highly absorbent: only a small amount is needed and it is ideal for binding the energy bites mixture.

Protein powder and colostrum powder are used in some of the fitness recipes in this book. These provide plenty of amino acids to support the recovery and repair of muscles after exercise and help to stabilize blood sugar levels, enabling you to train harder for longer.

Colostrum is the first milk produced by mammals and contains immunoglobulins, anti-microbial peptides and other bioactive molecules including growth factors to support a healthy immune system, aid the growth and repair of tissue, and maintain a healthy digestive tract. Now readily available as a supplement powder, it is popular with athletes before and after training.

If you cannot get hold of colostrum, you could use any protein powder instead – choose plain or vanilla according to taste. To keep the sugar content low, make sure you check your brand for any sweeteners it contains.

WET INGREDIENTS

Fresh veg, fruit and pulses add flavour, nutrients and moisture to energy bites. For the best results, choose whole fruits and canned beans and pulses such as chickpeas.

You can use these puréed or grated. Canned unsweetened pumpkin purée and apple purée are easily available or you can simply cook and purée your own. Frozen fruit also adds a wonderful creamy texture to bites.

Coconut oil is solid at room temperature, naturally dairy-free and has a delicious creamy texture. Used melted or softened, the oil helps bind the energy bites and adds a lovely rich taste. Coconut oil is a medium-chain fatty acid and is predominantly made up of lauric acid, known to support immune health.

Coconut milk and cream, or almond milk, are included in some of the recipes. These naturally dairy-free options add the necessary moisture to the bites, helping the mixture combine and stick together as well as adding healthy fats to the recipe. By including such fats, you help satisfy appetite and stabilize blood sugar levels, preventing energy crashes during the day.

Tahini (sesame seed paste) is rich in B vitamins, along with minerals, including magnesium, copper, calcium, phosphorus, manganese, iron and zinc. It provides amino acids and polyunsaturated essential fatty acids, giving a delicious silky texture.

Nut butters are also used in the recipes – select those without added sugars or sweeteners and watch the salt content. Better still, make your own from raw unsalted nuts (see recipe on page 22). Nut and seed butters can be used interchangeably in the recipes in this book.

Cacao butter is the natural fat from the cocoa bean. Free from dairy, gluten and sugar and solid at room temperature, it provides a creamy texture and helps energy bites to firm up once they are chilled.

FLAVOURINGS AND COATINGS

Ground cinnamon gives a lovely warming flavour. There are actually two different varieties of this spice – Ceylon and cassia. Where possible, choose Ceylon, which is the type associated with health benefits. Cinnamon has a very low GI, making it an ideal natural sweetener. It has also been studied for its benefits in balancing blood sugar and improving insulin sensitivity of cells.

Ginger, whether fresh root or ground, adds a lightly spiced flavour to energy bites. For a sweeter addition use stem ginger, which is sold in jars. Ginger is high in gingerols, a substance with powerful anti-inflammatory and antioxidant properties.

Lemon, lime or orange zest is a great way to add plenty of flavour to your bites. Choose organic unwaxed fruit.

Flavour extracts, such as vanilla and almond, can also be used to give a boost to energy bites. Choose natural extracts, which will have little to no sugar and normally a fresher, cleaner flavour. You can also use pure ground vanilla bean powder or vanilla paste, which are both sugar free.

Raw cacao powder is preferred over processed cocoa powder for the recipes in this book, being higher in antioxidants and minerals. It also has a richer, milder taste. But feel free to use the processed version if that is all you have available – you may just need to use a little less.

SUPERFOOD POWDERS

Lucuma powder
Made from Peruvian lucuma fruit that has been dried at low temperatures and milled into a fine powder, this low-glycaemic sweetener contains many nutrients including beta-carotene, iron, zinc, vitamin B3, calcium and protein. It also has a delicious maple-caramel taste.

Maca powder
A potent root from the Andes in Peru, maca has been used by cultures as a source of nourishment for thousands of years. Referred to as an adaptogenic herb, it has been studied for its ability to help the body adapt to stress. Popular as a superfood to help boost energy and performance, it has a lovely creamy, slightly nutty flavour.

Berry powders
Berries are prized for their nutrient density, and using berry powder further enhances the flavour and nutritional benefits of your bites. Use freeze-dried powders that retain the vital nutrients and flavour of the fresh fruit. You can find berry mixtures or use individual berry powders such as acai. These are low-glycaemic fruits packed with antioxidants and fibre.

Matcha green tea powder
Made from the whole leaf of the tea plant, matcha powder is packed with antioxidants including catechins, known for their anti-inflammatory properties. Matcha green tea has been shown to boost metabolism and burn calories, support detoxification and boost mood and concentration. As it is concentrated, you will only need one to three teaspoons in most recipes.

Supergreens powders
Chlorella, spirulina, wheatgrass and barley grass are just a few examples of green superfood powders. Packed with chlorophyll and antioxidants, these help to lower inflammation and support cleansing and detoxification of the body. Many, such as spirulina, are also rich in amino acids and essential fats as well as a vast array of vitamins and minerals, making them powerful energizing additions. As these are strong in flavour, use sparingly – just half to one teaspoon is normally sufficient.

WHY LOW SUGAR?

We are all becoming more aware of the harmful effects sugar has on the body. With rates of diabetes, insulin resistance and obesity rising, there are many reasons why we should cut down our intake. Added sugars (such as sucrose and many syrups) contain plenty of calories but no essential nutrients – they are what we term "empty" calories. Not only are they damaging to our waistline and our teeth, but more and more research is linking a high intake of sugars to long-term health conditions such as cancers, autoimmune diseases, diabetes, inflammatory conditions, heart disease and brain disorders.

Before sugar enters the bloodstream from the digestive tract, it is broken down into two simple sugars: glucose and fructose. Glucose can also be produced by our bodies and used as a fuel but fructose is not produced in any significant amount and our bodies can only metabolize it through the liver. This is not a problem if we eat only a little (e.g. in a piece of fruit) or if we have been exercising hard and our bodies can quickly use it for energy. The trouble is many foods contain so much fructose from added sugars that the body cannot use it and it is converted into fat in the liver.

Sugars are found naturally in foods such as fruits, vegetables, grains and as lactose in milk products. The main concern, however, is around added sugars, usually in the form of sucrose (table sugar), syrups and high-fructose corn syrup. It is estimated that a half of our intake comes from everyday foods such as ketchup, salad dressings and bread.

That's not to say you should avoid whole fresh fruit – especially the lower glycaemic fruits such as berries, avocado, cherries and citrus fruits. The glycaemic index (GI) measures how blood sugar levels react to carbohydrate-based food and drink. Pure glucose (100 GI) is used as a reference of scale. Foods with a low GI, such as most fruit and vegetables, slowly raise blood glucose levels. They are packed with antioxidants, vitamins and minerals and their fibre content helps slow down the rate at which the sugars are digested and metabolized, avoiding sudden surges in blood sugar levels. However, dried fruit, which forms the base of most energy bites on the market, is a very concentrated form of sugar and fructose and it is easy to eat far too much. Some of our recipes include dried fruit, but only a low amount.

NATURAL WAYS TO SWEETEN

Rather than relying on syrups, sugar and dried fruit for sweetness, some of the recipes in this book make use of vegetables and fruits that are naturally sweet – for example, pumpkin, carrot and butternut squash are starchy, sweet vegetables. Other recipes use whole fruits like apples, pears and plums or berries. In some cases, you can add sweetness using spices such as cinnamon or powders like lucuma. Where you need more sweetness, here are a few safer options you can try.

Xylitol and erythritol are sweeteners known as sugar alcohols, and they can be used interchangeably. Naturally derived, typically from corn and birch, they are much lower in calories than regular sugar and do not upset blood sugar levels. They are available in granular form and can be used to replace normal sugar in recipes at a 1:1 ratio. Excess xylitol has been known to cause digestive upsets in some people.

Stevia is a natural low-calorie sweetener available in liquid or granular form. Extracted from the leaves of the plant *Stevia rebaudiana*, it is incredibly sweet and you need much less of it than regular sugar in recipes as 1 teaspoon of stevia is the equivalent flavour of 200g of sugar. Stevia contains virtually no calories, has a low glycaemic index and is fructose free.

Yacon syrup comes from the yacon tuber, an Andean crop. The syrup tastes a bit like molasses, but has a low glycaemic score (between 1 and 5). As it does still contain fructose (around 40 per cent), it is best used sparingly and more as a flavouring rather than a sweetener.

Rice malt syrup is made from fermented brown rice and has a lower fructose content but it is still high in calories so again, use sparingly. Check labels to make sure rice and water are the only ingredients. While other syrups such as maple syrup or honey can be used, these are higher glycaemic sweeteners.

MAKING ENERGY BITES

Energy bites are very simple to make. Many of the recipes make use of a standard food processor or blender for speed but it's often possible to make them by hand in a mixing bowl, finely chopping all the dry ingredients first.

All the recipes include a mixture of wet and dry ingredients, which are outlined over the next few pages. This not only helps them bind and hold together but also provides a good balance of protein, healthy fats and carbohydrates. You can then add optional extras to provide flavour or nutritional benefits. Here are three basic steps to creating your own energy bites:

1. Start with your base of dry ingredients – this could include rolled oats, ground-up nuts and seeds or protein powder. If you are gluten free, substitute gluten-free oats for oats or use an alternative such as quinoa, millet or buckwheat flakes.

2. Next, mix in the wet, sticky ingredients. This is what will hold it all together. Choose from nut butters, grated or puréed fruit and vegetables, cooked beans, melted coconut oil or cacao butter or very occasionally a drop of yacon syrup or fruit concentrate. You can also use yogurt, coconut cream, cream cheese and almond milk or other milk alternatives.

3. Now for the extras: these are optional but provide texture and flavour as well as additional nutrients. Examples include coconut, finely chopped nuts, chocolate chips, a little dried fruit, natural extracts such as vanilla or almond, spices and cacao or superfood powders. This is where you can also adjust the sweetness and, if needed, add a little natural sweetener to suit your taste. Either add to the mix or roll the energy bites in your extra flavourings.

MAKE YOUR OWN NUT BUTTER

While nut and seed butters are now widely available, if you're a big fan of them you may find it cheaper to buy nuts and seeds in bulk and make your own. You'll also get the feel-good factor from doing it yourself! You will need either a high-speed blender or a food processor and some clean jars or containers.

1. Choose raw and unsalted shelled nuts. You can use just one type of nut (peanuts, almonds, cashews and macadamias work well) or a mixture. As a rough guide, 250g nuts will give 1 cup of nut butter but it depends on the nuts used.

2. Simply place the nuts in a food processor and blend on high until the mixture is smooth and creamy. You may have to stop from time to time to scrape down the sides of the container. You should not need to add any liquid or oil as the nuts will naturally start to release their own oils as you process.

3. Store your nut butter in an airtight container or glass jar in the fridge for up to 2–3 weeks. You can also freeze nut butter for up to 3 months.

ADDITIONAL FLAVOUR

There are many ways you can jazz up homemade nut butters. You can turn them into choco-nut spread by adding raw cacao powder along with a little almond milk or coconut milk to form a thick chocolate paste. Nut butters are also delicious with other added superfoods – try lucuma powder or maca powder for a mild caramel flavour. If you like a sweeter nut butter then add a little yacon syrup, finely ground xylitol or a few drops of stevia. Make use too of natural extracts like vanilla or spices such as cinnamon for additional flavour.

There is also no reason why you cannot combine nuts and seeds together. Alternatively try using half unsweetened coconut flakes and half nuts for a creamy spread.

ACTIVATED NUTS

If you find nuts and seeds difficult to digest, you could try using activated nuts instead. These are simply soaked and dried nuts or seeds which are blended in the same way as regular nuts to make nut butters. You can either do this yourself or buy activated nuts.

When you soak and then dry them it activates enzymes to start the sprouting process and this makes them easier to digest. The activation process also produces a crunchier texture. Almonds, walnuts, pecans, pumpkin and sunflower seeds are the best to uses as the oily nuts like macadamia tend to need more soaking and often go too soggy.

To soak your nuts, simply place them in a bowl of fresh water and leave overnight. Drain, then spread out on a baking tray and dry in the oven for 12–24 hours at the lowest setting possible (ideally less than 45°C). You can also dry the nuts in a dehydrator if you have one. Once fully dried, store them in an airtight container in the fridge or freezer until needed.

FITNESS BOOSTERS

These recipes have been designed specifically to be eaten before or after your workout. Combining protein and carbohydrates for a good energy boost, some of these bites are slightly higher in fruit too, to help replace stores of glycogen (a type of glucose that fuels tired muscles) after exercising.

MATCHA PROTEIN BITES

Cacao butter gives these green nuggets a creamy texture and rich flavour while the protein powder keeps them grain free, which is perfect if you are following a paleo or gluten free diet. Matcha green tea has very high antioxidant levels (nearly 10 times stronger than green tea). Its stimulant and metabolism-boosting properties are ideal for optimal performance as well as for recovery.

Place the stevia or xylitol in a blender or food processor and grind until very fine.

Add the nut butter, matcha powder, sea salt, vanilla and melted cacao butter to the food processor and combine.

Add the protein powder and process to form a dough. If the mixture is too soft, add another spoonful of protein powder. Chill the dough in the fridge for 15-20 minutes to firm up slightly. Take small spoonfuls of the mixture and roll into walnut-sized balls.

Place a little matcha green tea powder and/or protein powder on a plate. Roll the balls in the mixture to coat. Keep in the fridge until required.

MAKES 20

15g granulated stevia or 30g xylitol/erythritol

115g macadamia nut butter or cashew nut butter

1 tbsp matcha green tea powder

Pinch of sea salt

1 tbsp vanilla extract

60g cacao butter, melted

60-80g chocolate or vanilla protein powder

Matcha green tea powder and/or protein powder to coat

PER BITE:

Calories 81kcal

Fat 6.2g (saturates 0.5g)

Carbohydrates 1.3g

Sugars 1g

Protein 4.4g

BERRY BLISS
FITNESS BITES

MAKES 20

90g sunflower seeds

30g pumpkin seeds

30g flaxseeds

**60g vanilla protein
powder or
collagen powder**

**40g tahini or nut
butter**

**1 tsp granulated
stevia**

**Juice and zest of
1 lemon**

**30g dried berries
(cherries,
cranberries or
raisins work well)**

**1 tbsp acai berry
powder or other
berry superfood
powder, to coat
(optional)**

These delicious bliss balls are perfect for a
post-workout treat. The berries provide plenty of
antioxidants, which have been shown to reduce
muscle soreness and speed up recovery after a
hard workout. The combination of protein and carbs
is ideal for replenishing stored glycogen which can
be depleted after training, and the protein supports
muscle repair.

Place the seeds in a food processor and process
until fine. Add the remaining ingredients except
for the dried berries and acai berry powder, and
process to combine. Add the berries and pulse to
break them up but still keep some texture. Add a
little water if needed to form a soft dough.

Take walnut-sized pieces of the dough and roll into
balls. Dust in a little acai berry powder if wished.
Store in the fridge for up to 1 week.

PER BITE:

Calories 77kcal

**Fat 5.1g (saturates
0.6g)**

Carbohydrates 3.2g

Sugars 1.2g

Protein 3.8g

When you soak and then dry them it activates enzymes to start the sprouting process and this makes them easier to digest. The activation process also produces a crunchier texture. Almonds, walnuts, pecans, pumpkin and sunflower seeds are the best to uses as the oily nuts like macadamia tend to need more soaking and often go too soggy.

To soak your nuts, simply place them in a bowl of fresh water and leave overnight. Drain, then spread out on a baking tray and dry in the oven for 12–24 hours at the lowest setting possible (ideally less than 45°C). You can also dry the nuts in a dehydrator if you have one. Once fully dried, store them in an airtight container in the fridge or freezer until needed.

FITNESS BOOSTERS

These recipes have been designed specifically to be eaten before or after your workout. Combining protein and carbohydrates for a good energy boost, some of these bites are slightly higher in fruit too, to help replace stores of glycogen (a type of glucose that fuels tired muscles) after exercising.

MATCHA PROTEIN BITES

MAKES 20

15g granulated stevia or 30g xylitol/erythritol

115g macadamia nut butter or cashew nut butter

1 tbsp matcha green tea powder

Pinch of sea salt

1 tbsp vanilla extract

60g cacao butter, melted

60-80g chocolate or vanilla protein powder

Matcha green tea powder and/or protein powder to coat

PER BITE:

Calories 81kcal

Fat 6.2g (saturates 0.5g)

Carbohydrates 1.3g

Sugars 1g

Protein 4.4g

Cacao butter gives these green nuggets a creamy texture and rich flavour while the protein powder keeps them grain free, which is perfect if you are following a paleo or gluten free diet. Matcha green tea has very high antioxidant levels (nearly 10 times stronger than green tea). Its stimulant and metabolism-boosting properties are ideal for optimal performance as well as for recovery.

Place the stevia or xylitol in a blender or food processor and grind until very fine.

Add the nut butter, matcha powder, sea salt, vanilla and melted cacao butter to the food processor and combine.

Add the protein powder and process to form a dough. If the mixture is too soft, add another spoonful of protein powder. Chill the dough in the fridge for 15-20 minutes to firm up slightly. Take small spoonfuls of the mixture and roll into walnut-sized balls.

Place a little matcha green tea powder and/or protein powder on a plate. Roll the balls in the mixture to coat. Keep in the fridge until required.

BERRY BLISS FITNESS BITES

These delicious bliss balls are perfect for a post-workout treat. The berries provide plenty of antioxidants, which have been shown to reduce muscle soreness and speed up recovery after a hard workout. The combination of protein and carbs is ideal for replenishing stored glycogen which can be depleted after training, and the protein supports muscle repair.

MAKES 20

90g sunflower seeds

30g pumpkin seeds

30g flaxseeds

60g vanilla protein powder or collagen powder

40g tahini or nut butter

1 tsp granulated stevia

Juice and zest of 1 lemon

30g dried berries (cherries, cranberries or raisins work well)

1 tbsp acai berry powder or other berry superfood powder, to coat (optional)

Place the seeds in a food processor and process until fine. Add the remaining ingredients except for the dried berries and acai berry powder, and process to combine. Add the berries and pulse to break them up but still keep some texture. Add a little water if needed to form a soft dough.

Take walnut-sized pieces of the dough and roll into balls. Dust in a little acai berry powder if wished. Store in the fridge for up to 1 week.

PER BITE:

Calories 77kcal

Fat 5.1g (saturates 0.6g)

Carbohydrates 3.2g

Sugars 1.2g

Protein 3.8g

PALEO BLUEBERRY MUFFIN BITES

These berry bites are packed with protein and the coconut flour makes them gluten free and suitable for those on a paleo diet. Coconut flour is also higher in fibre and low in carbs, meaning it won't spike your blood sugar levels like grains do – so these bites are ideal for a pre-workout snack to keep energy levels high during training. Coconut flour also contains medium-chain triglycerides which the body can preferentially use as a fuel too – perfect for boosting your performance.

Place the coconut flour, protein powder, sea salt, stevia and cinnamon in a mixing bowl or food processor. Combine well. Add the blueberries and tahini, and then add enough milk to form a stiff dough. Do not overprocess.

Form the mixture into bite-sized balls, then refrigerate for at least 30 minutes to firm.

Eat immediately, or store in the fridge for up to 1 week. Alternatively, you can freeze them for up to 3 months.

MAKES 16

60g coconut flour

30g protein powder (vanilla or berry flavour)

Pinch of sea salt

1 tsp granulated stevia

$\frac{1}{2}$ tsp ground cinnamon

50g dried blueberries

1 tbsp tahini

100ml coconut milk or almond milk

PER BITE:

Calories 44kcal

Fat 1.5g (saturates 0.6g)

Carbohydrates 4.5g

Sugars 2.3g

Protein 2.4g

FIG WALNUT BITES

These are similar in taste to the popular fig roll biscuits. As they contain a higher amount of dried fruit than other energy balls in this book, use them as an energy boost pre- or post-workout.

Place the dried figs with the vanilla, orange juice and salt in a food processor and blend to form a thick purée. Add the oats and walnuts and process again to form a soft dough. Keep some texture in the mix.

Take bite-sized pieces and roll into balls. Roll the balls in the chopped toasted nuts to coat. Store in the fridge for up to 1 week.

MAKES 20

100g ready-to-eat
   dried figs
1 tbsp vanilla extract
3 tbsp orange juice
Pinch of salt
50g porridge oats
75g walnuts, toasted
   and chopped
60g chopped toasted
   nuts, to coat

PER BITE:
Calories 60kcal
Fat 3.9g (saturates
   0.4g)
Carbohydrates 4.4g
Sugars 2.8g
Protein 1.4g

STRAWBERRY CREAM PROTEIN BITES

MAKES 24

90g colostrum powder or vanilla protein powder

65g desiccated coconut

1 tbsp ground flaxseed

50g cashew nut butter

75g coconut oil, softened

30g xylitol or erythritol

1 tsp vanilla extract

120g frozen strawberries

Pinch of sea salt

Colostrum powder or desiccated coconut, to coat

PER BITE:

Calories 81kcal

Fat 6.2g (saturates 0.5g)

Carbohydrates 1.3g

Sugars 1g

Protein 4.4g

Naturally creamy thanks to the addition of colostrum or vanilla protein powder, this is an ideal after-workout snack, rich in both protein and carbohydrates. Using strawberries adds plenty of vitamin C and antioxidants which are perfect for speeding up recovery after exercise. The flaxseed adds fibre and supports digestive health, and together with the protein keeps blood sugar levels balanced.

Place the colostrum, coconut and flaxseed in a food processor and process until smooth. Add the nut butter, coconut oil (softened, not melted), xylitol and vanilla and process to combine.

Add the frozen strawberries and a pinch of salt and process until the mixture comes together.

Take small pieces of the mixture and roll into small balls. Roll them in a little desiccated coconut or colostrum powder.

Store in the fridge until required. These will keep in the fridge for 4–5 days. Alternatively, you can freeze them for up to 3 months.

RED VELVET BITES

Beetroot and chocolate are a brilliant combination. Beetroot contains nitrates, which the body converts to nitric oxide, in turn boosting blood flow and improving oxygenation of the body, allowing you to exercise harder for longer. Dark chocolate is rich in a substance called epicatechin, a nutrient rich flavanol that also increases nitric oxide production.

MAKES 14

- 60g cooked beetroot (without vinegar)
- 60g pitted cherries, raspberries or strawberries – fresh or frozen
- 60g canned coconut cream (see page 70 for instructions)
- 150g dark chocolate, broken into pieces
- 2 tsp acai berry powder
- Berry powder, crushed freeze-dried berries or raw cacao, to coat

Place the beetroot, raspberries and coconut cream in a blender and purée until smooth. Transfer to a small pan with the chocolate and heat gently, stirring all the time until the chocolate has melted. Pour the mixture into a bowl and chill in the fridge for 3–4 hours or freeze for 1 hour to harden.

Once firm, roll teaspoonfuls of the mixture into small balls with your hands. Roll in berry powder, freeze-dried berries or cacao powder to coat.

Freeze or place the bites in the fridge to harden. They will keep in the fridge for 1 week or in the freezer for 3 months.

PER BITE:

Calories 80kcal

Fat 5.6g (saturates 3.8g)

Carbohydrates 5.9g

Sugars 1.2g

Protein 1.5g

CHEWY BANANA BREAD BITES

MAKES 24

75g banana chips

60g walnuts

75g dry buckwheat groats, soaked in water for 1 hour then drained

50g almond nut butter

2 tsp ground cinnamon

Pinch of sea salt

2 tsp vanilla extract

2 tsp coconut oil, softened

These are a slightly sweet bite with the addition of the banana chips. Buckwheat is a nutritious gluten free grain, rich in antioxidants such as rutin, which can help strengthen blood vessels and improve circulation. It is also a naturally rich source of protein and fibre to help balance blood sugar and keep you feeling fuller for longer. And it's perfect for energizing the body too, being rich in B vitamins and magnesium.

Place the banana chips, walnuts and buckwheat in a food processor and process briefly to break up the chips and nuts.

Add the remaining ingredients and process briefly so the mixture comes together.

Form the mixture into small balls. Keep in the fridge for up to 1 week.

PER BITE:

Calories 63kcal

Fat 4.2g (saturates 1.5g)

Carbohydrates 4.6g

Sugars 1.3g

Protein 1.4g

KALE AND APPLE SUPERGREEN BITES

These green nuggets are rich and creamy and no one would guess you've added kale! The addition of raw cacao gives them a wonderfully indulgent texture. Low levels of magnesium are known to lead to reduced physical performance, muscle cramps and soreness after workouts so the greens here provide plenty of magnesium to support energy production and recovery.

Place all the ingredients in a food processor and blend to form a soft dough.

Take small walnut-sized pieces of the mixture and roll into balls. Roll in wheatgrass powder or crushed nuts.

These bites can be frozen for up to 3 months if wished. Once defrosted, they will keep in the fridge for up to 1 week.

MAKES 28

- 100g ground almonds
- 50g desiccated coconut
- Handful of kale leaves
- 60g dried apple or pear pieces
- 50g raw cacao butter, melted
- 2 tsp wheatgrass powder or other supergreens powder
- 60g vanilla protein powder
- 2 tbsp almond milk or coconut cream
- Wheatgrass powder or finely chopped pistachio nuts, to coat

PER BITE:

Calories 65kcal

Fat 5g (saturates 1.1g)

Carbohydrates 1.7g

Sugars 1.5g

Protein 2.9g

THREE

ON
THE RUN

A selection of energy bites for everyday eating,
whether it's a speedy breakfast, an office snack,
lunchboxes or an afternoon pick-me-up. With all sorts
of flavours, from banana to apple to coconut, here are
recipes that are ideal for busy people.

APPLE CINNAMON BREAKFAST BITES

MAKES 18

30g dried apples
1 tsp vanilla extract
30g lucuma powder
65g sunflower seeds
½ apple, peeled
15g ground flaxseed
2 tsp ground
    cinnamon
Pinch of sea salt
50g rolled oats
Powdered xylitol and
    cinnamon, to coat

Fancy an alternative for breakfast? These delicious oat nuggets will energize you in the morning. Crammed with plenty of slow-releasing carbohydrates, fibre and protein, they make an ideal start to the day. The lucuma gives a great flavour and sweetness.

Place all the ingredients except the oats, powdered xylitol and cinnamon in a food processor and blitz to break up the seeds. Add the oats and pulse briefly to bring the mixture together, keeping some texture.

Form into walnut-sized balls. Roll each ball in the powdered xylitol and cinnamon mixture. Store in the fridge for up to 1 week·

PER BITE:
Calories 50kcal
Fat 2.3g (saturates
    0.3g)
Carbohydrates 5.2g
Sugars 1.5g
Protein 1.5g

MOCHA BREAKFAST OATMEAL BITES

These coffee-flavoured bites are a great grab-and-go breakfast option. Naturally sweetened with banana they are also packed with fibre to help stabilize blood sugar levels.

Place the oats, flaxseed, coffee and cacao powder in a food processor and briefly process to combine. Add the remaining ingredients and process until the mixture comes together to form a soft dough. Try not to overprocess so you keep some texture.

Take small walnut-sized pieces of the dough and roll into balls. Dust in a little ground coffee mixed with cacao powder if wished.

Refrigerate the bites until required. They will keep for at least 1 week in the fridge.

MAKES 18

50g porridge oats

30g ground flaxseed or chia seeds

2 tsp ground coffee (instant or fresh)

30g raw cacao powder

1 tbsp vanilla extract

75g tahini

½ large banana

Pinch of sea salt

Ground coffee mixed with cacao powder, to coat (optional)

PER BITE:

Calories 58kcal

Fat 3.5g (saturates 0.5g)

Carbohydrates 3.9g

Sugars 0.6g

Protein 1.9g

APRICOT AND COCONUT BITES

MAKES 15

- **90g desiccated coconut**
- **1 tbsp coconut oil**
- **Zest of 1 orange**
- **1 tbsp ground chia seeds**
- **2 fresh stoned apricots (about 100g)**
- **30g desiccated coconut or 60g melted dark chocolate, to coat**

This simple recipe uses just a handful of ingredients. Using fresh apricots rather than dried reduces the overall sugar content while still providing natural sweetness and fibre. The chia seeds help to bind the mixture. You can coat these in desiccated coconut or, for a more indulgent treat, dip in chocolate.

Line a baking tray with baking parchment. Place all the ingredients in a food processor and process to combine, but keep a little texture in the mixture.

Roll tablespoons of the mixture into balls. You can either roll the balls in the coconut or freeze until firm and then coat in melted chocolate.

Place the bites on the baking tray and freeze for 1 hour to harden. Store in the fridge for up to 1 week or keep in the freezer.

PER BITE:

Calories 56kcal

Fat 4.7g (saturates 3.8g)

Carbohydrates 1.2g

Sugars 0.8g

Protein 1.4g

MAKES 14

60g courgette, grated

30g apple purée

½ apple, grated

1 tsp ground cinnamon

30g almond nut butter or other nut butter

30g coconut flour

50g porridge oats

2 tsp chia seeds

1 tsp vanilla extract

COURGETTE AND APPLE CAKE BITES

These delicious green bites are naturally sweetened with apple and have a warming cinnamon flavour reminiscent of courgette cake. The coconut flour gives a unique texture and helps to bind the mixture.

Place all the ingredients in a food processor and process just until the mixture starts to come together to form a soft dough.

Take walnut-sized pieces and roll into balls. Store in the fridge for up to 1 week.

PER BITE:

Calories 46kcal

Fat 2g (saturates 0.5g)

Carbohydrates 4.6g

Sugars 0.9g

Protein 1.5g

PLUM CRUMBLE BITES

These light, crunchy bites combine all the ingredients of a fruit crumble in one mouthful. Using fresh plums rather than dried fruit keeps the sugar content low but adds plenty of fibre to support digestive health. The addition of protein powder makes these bites ideal for stabilizing blood sugar levels, preventing dips in energy through the day.

Place the plum, nut butter, vanilla and stevia in a food processor and blend to form a thick paste. Add the protein powder, almonds, oats and cinnamon and process again to combine.

Pulse in the granola or oats to combine but leave some crumbly texture.

Scoop the mixture out with a teaspoon and roll into balls.

Store in the fridge for up to 1 week or freeze for up to 3 months. You can eat the bites straight from the freezer or place in the fridge to defrost.

MAKES 22

1 medium plum, stoned, about 70g

100g almond butter or other nut butter

1 tsp vanilla extract

1 tsp granulated stevia

50g vanilla protein powder

40g ground almonds

30g porridge oats, quinoa flakes or buckwheat flakes

1 tsp ground cinnamon

30g granola or additional porridge oats

PER BITE:

Calories 62kcal

Fat 3.8g (saturates 0.5g)

Carbohydrates 2.7g

Sugars 0.7g

Protein 3.9g

PISTACHIO CRANBERRY BITES

These delicious nutty bites are rich in protein and healthy fats. Use any nut butter you like but try to choose one without additives and sweeteners. Pistachios are a great source of monounsaturated heart-healthy fats, vitamin E and carotenes, helping to contribute to glowing skin.

MAKES 36

- 125g shelled pistachio nuts
- 1 tbsp ground chia seeds
- 30g xylitol or erythritol
- 60g almonds
- 100g almond nut butter or other nut butter
- 1 tbsp vanilla extract
- 60g dried cranberries

Place the pistachios, chia seeds, xylitol and almonds in a food processor and process until fine. Add the nut butter, vanilla and half the cranberries and continue to process until the mixture comes together. Add the remaining cranberries and pulse to break up.

Take pieces of the dough and roll into little balls. Store in the fridge until required. They will keep for 1-2 weeks.

PER BITE:

Calories 58kcal

Fat 4.4g (saturates 0.6g)

Carbohydrates 2.2g

Sugars 1.5g

Protein 2g

BLACKCURRANT BLISS BITES

MAKES 14

60g walnuts

60g pecans

30g raw cacao powder

1 tbsp freeze-dried blackcurrant powder or other berry powder

Pinch of sea salt

1 tbsp blueberry or cherry juice concentrate

50g Greek yogurt

Crushed nuts, to coat (optional)

Blackcurrants are a seasonal fruit but you can find freeze-dried blackcurrant powder (and other berry powders) any time of year – a great way to add flavour, antioxidants and vitamin C. These bites are sweetened with a little blueberry or cherry concentrate – if unavailable you could use apple purée. The walnuts add plant-based omega-3 fats along with protein and give these balls a rich taste when combined with the raw cacao powder.

Place the walnuts, pecans and cacao powder in a food processor and combine until the nuts are finely ground. Add the blackcurrant powder and sea salt, then pour in the juice and yogurt and process to combine.

Take teaspoons of the mixture and roll into small balls. Roll in crushed nuts if wished. Store in the fridge for up to 1 week.

PER BITE:

Calories 80kcal

Fat 6.6g (saturates 0.9g)

Carbohydrates 2.8g

Sugars 1.1g

Protein 1.8g

KEY LIME PIE BITES

MAKES 18

30g xylitol or 15g
   granulated stevia
125g macadamia
   nuts
35g desiccated
   coconut
2 tsp wheatgrass
   powder or
   supergreens
   powder
Zest and juice of
   1 lime
Pinch of sea salt
1 tsp coconut oil,
   softened
Powdered xylitol
   mixed with a little
   lime zest, to coat

Lime and coconut is a delicious combination. The
sharpness of the lime is a wonderful contrast to the
creamy texture of these little bites. Macadamia nuts
are packed with anti-inflammatory fats and rich in B
vitamins, manganese and magnesium, which are all
important for energy production.

Place the xylitol in a food processor and blend
until really fine. Add the nuts and coconut and
continue to process until fine.

Add the green powder, lime zest and juice and
sea salt and process until the mixture forms
a soft dough. Add the coconut oil to help the
mixture come together.

Scoop out bite-sized pieces and roll into balls.
Roll in the powdered xylitol mixed with lime zest.

Store the balls in the fridge until required,
or keep them in the freezer for up to
3 months.

PER BITE:
Calories 73kcal
Fat 6.6g (saturates
   1.8g)
Carbohydrates 2.1g
Sugars 0.4g
Protein 0.9g

ORANGE GOJI ENERGY BITES

These deliciously fruity bites make a tasty pick-me-up. Using the whole fruit in the mix means you include all the valuable fibre which helps balance blood sugar and keeps you feeling fuller for longer. Goji berries are an excellent source of vitamin C and antioxidants.

Place the coconut, ground almonds, salt, nut butter and satsumas in a food processor and process until the mixture comes together. Add the rice cereal and goji berries and continue to process until the mixture comes together but there is still texture – do not overprocess.

Take spoonfuls of the mixture and roll into balls. Place on a tray or plate. Refrigerate until needed. These will keep in the fridge for 1 week.

MAKES 24

30g desiccated coconut

60g ground almonds

Pinch of sea salt

65g cashew nut or peanut nut butter

2 satsumas, peeled

50g puffed brown rice cereal (unsweetened)

30g goji berries

PER BITE:

Calories 50kcal

Fat 2.5g (saturates 0.9g)

Carbohydrates 3.4g

Sugars 1.4g

Protein 3.1g

MANGO AND TURMERIC BITES

MAKES 25

150g porridge oats
    (gluten free if
    preferred)
30g coconut flour
1 tbsp granulated
    stevia
½ tsp turmeric
½ tsp ground
    cinnamon
130g mango chunks
    (roughly half a
    large mango)
1 tsp vanilla extract
75g cashew butter
    or other nut
    butter
1 tbsp coconut oil
Extra granulated
    stevia and
    turmeric, to coat

Turmeric is a fabulous super spice – known for its anti-inflammatory and antioxidant properties – and combines well with the sweetness of mango. Using oats is a great way to add plenty of soluble fibre, protein and B vitamins to keep the body energized through the day.

Place all the ingredients in a food processor and blend together to form a soft dough.

Take spoonfuls of the mixture and shape into small balls. Roll the balls in a mixture of granulated stevia and turmeric to coat.

Place in the fridge until required, for up to 1 week. The bites can also be frozen for up to 3 months.

PER BITE:

Calories 55cal

Fat 2.6g (saturates 0.8g)

Carbohydrates 5.4g

Sugars 0.6g

Protein 1.8g

FOUR

GIFTS AND INDULGENCES

Now for the fun stuff – the bites in this chapter are
perfect for special occasions. Simply package in a jar
or box, add ribbon and a label and voilà – a gorgeous
homemade gift. This section also includes slightly
more indulgent bites, ideal for sweet cravings or to
have after dinner instead of dessert.

CARROT CAKE BITES

MAKES 24

50g raisins

1 tsp vanilla extract

**30g ground almonds
or flaxseed**

**1 tbsp xylitol or
erythritol**

**60g unsweetened
coconut flakes**

1 tbsp coconut oil

75g walnuts

2 tbsp coconut flour

**1 tsp ground
cinnamon**

**75g carrot, finely
grated**

Pinch of sea salt

2 tbsp apple purée

Inspired by carrot cake, these delicious little nuggets are creamy and sweet with the addition of apple purée and raisins. Walnuts provide essential omega-3 fats, known to lower inflammation and keep the skin glowing.

Place all the ingredients in a food processor and process to form a dough. Keep some texture in the mixture so do not overprocess.

Take bite-size pieces of the dough and roll into balls. Store in the fridge for up to 1 week.

For a thoughtful homemade gift, place the energy bites in a jar, and decorate with a ribbon or hand-written label.

PER BITE:

Calories 66kcal

**Fat 4.8g (saturates
2.1g)**

Carbohydrates 3.6g

Sugars 2.2g

Protein 1.2g

PEANUT CRISPIES

MAKES 24

60g coconut oil

50g yacon syrup or
    rice malt syrup

60g peanut butter
    or other nut
    butter

30g raw cacao
    powder

40g desiccated
    coconut

30g puffed rice

These are similar to the traditional children's favourite, chocolate crispies, but much better for you. Yacon syrup is a healthier sweetener with a lower glycaemic index and high content of the dietary fibre inulin, making it ideal for supporting digestive health. If you can't get hold of it, use rice malt syrup instead. Any nut butter can be used instead of peanut butter.

Gently heat the coconut oil, yacon syrup and peanut butter in a saucepan and stir until melted. Turn off the heat. Add the cacao powder, coconut and puffed rice and stir well to coat.

Scoop out spoonfuls of the mixture, shape into small balls using two teaspoons and place into mini paper cases. Refrigerate for 1 hour until set. These will keep in the fridge for 1–2 weeks.

PER BITE:

Calories 64kcal

Fat 5g (saturates
    3.4g)

Carbohydrates 2.9g

Sugars 0.7g

Protein 1.2g

MINT CHOC CHIP CHLORELLA BITES

These are a healthy version of chocolate cookie dough. The green superfood powder is optional but gives the little bites a lovely green colour as well as being incredibly nutrient rich, containing B vitamins, iron, magnesium and antioxidants.

Place the cashew nuts, coconut flour, chlorella, protein powder or cacao powder and stevia in a food processor and process until fine.

Add the nut butter, syrup and peppermint extract to taste. Process until the mixture begins to form a soft dough. Add in the chocolate chips and almond milk and process until the mixture comes together.

Take small pieces of the dough and roll into balls. Place in the fridge to harden for about 30 minutes. Eat within 1–2 weeks.

MAKES 32

125g cashew nuts

30g coconut flour

1 tbsp chlorella powder or other supergreens powder

30g chocolate protein powder or raw cacao powder

15g granulated stevia, or to taste

160g almond nut butter or peanut butter

40g yacon syrup, rice malt syrup or honey

½ tsp peppermint extract, or to taste

60g dark chocolate chips or raw cacao nibs

2 tbsp almond milk

PER BITE:

Calories 77kcal

Fat 5.3g (saturates 1.3g)

Carbohydrates 3.2g

Sugars 1.1g

Protein 3.4g

HAZELNUT AND CHOCOLATE BITES

MAKES 22

- 125g hazelnuts
- 50g raw cacao powder
- 50g erythritol or xylitol
- 120g hazelnut butter or other nut butter
- 70g coconut cream (see page 70 for instructions)
- Chopped toasted hazelnuts, to coat

Wonderfully rich, these bites are packed with protein thanks to the addition of nuts and nut butter. Using coconut cream gives these bites a creamy texture and helps to keep you feeling satisfied by stabilizing blood sugar levels.

Place the hazelnuts, cacao powder and erythritol in a food processor and process until the hazelnuts are very fine. Add the nut butter and coconut cream, and process to form a soft dough.

Take spoonfuls of the mixture and roll into balls. Place the toasted hazelnuts on a plate and roll the balls in them to coat.

Decorate a tray of energy bites for a moreish and indulgent dessert for parties. They will also keep in the fridge for up to 1 week.

PER BITE:
Calories 104kcal
Fat 7.8g (saturates 1.8g)
Carbohydrates 4.6g
Sugars 0.6g
Protein 3g

MACA CHOCOLATE TRUFFLE BITES

MAKES 18

100ml almond milk

70g coconut oil,
    softened

150g plain chocolate
    chips or grated
    chocolate

30g xylitol

1 tbsp maca powder

1 tbsp lucuma
    powder

1 tsp vanilla extract

Extra maca or
    lucuma powder,
    to coat

Give these indulgent treats as a gift instead of a box of chocolates. The bites include maca, a popular superfood that give you a sustained energy boost through the day. It also supports energy levels and adrenal health. Using xylitol helps to keep the overall sugar content low.

Place the almond milk in a saucepan and bring to the simmer, then turn off the heat. Place all the other ingredients in a blender or food processor. Pour over the hot milk and blend until the mixture becomes a thick smooth batter. Spoon the mixture into a bowl and chill in the fridge for 1 hour until firm.

Using a spoon, roll the mixture into small truffles. Place the maca or lucuma powder on a plate and roll the truffles in the powder. Place on a plate and keep in the fridge until required.

These will keep in the fridge for up to 1 week.

PER BITE:

Calories 90kcal

Fat 6.3g (saturates
    4.8g)

Carbohydrates 7.7g

Sugars 5.1g

Protein 0.6g

CHOCOLATE AND COCONUT BITES

MAKES 24

125g coconut cream
(see note in
recipe intro)

2 tbsp yacon syrup,
maple syrup or
rice malt syrup

2 tbsp coconut oil

100g desiccated
coconut

Pinch of sea salt

200g chocolate
chips (use sugar-
free, dairy-free
chocolate if
you're vegan)

1 tsp coconut oil

A delicious mini morsel. For the coconut cream, chill an unopened can of full-fat coconut milk in the fridge for a few hours before using – the cream sets at the top of the can, making it easier to scoop out. Save the rest of the can to use in smoothies.

Place the coconut cream, syrup and coconut oil in a saucepan over a low heat. Stir until combined. Remove the pan from the heat. Place the desiccated coconut and salt in a food processor and blitz until fine. Add to the pan and stir in. Transfer the mixture to a bowl and place in the fridge for an hour to firm up.

Shape the mixture into walnut-sized balls. Place on a baking tray lined with greaseproof paper. Freeze for 30 minutes to firm up.

Place the chocolate chips and coconut oil in a pan and melt gently, stirring. Dip each ball into the chocolate with a fork and place back on the tray. Return to the freezer to firm up. Dip the balls in melted chocolate a second time and return to the freezer to set.

The bites will keep in the fridge for 1–2 weeks.

PER BITE:

Calories 90kcal

Fat 7.4g (saturates
5.7g)

Carbohydrates 4.1g

Sugars 0.8g

Protein 1.3g

PECAN PUMPKIN NUGGETS

The combination of pecans and pumpkin purée with winter spices makes these nuggets perfect autumn treats. The yacon syrup gives them a molasses-like taste but you can omit this and use a dash of milk or almond milk instead to bind.

Place the nuts and seeds in a food processor and process until the nuts are finely ground. Add the remaining ingredients, except the chocolate chips, cinnamon and xylitol, and process to form a dough.

Add in the chocolate chips and pulse to combine. Take bite-sized pieces of the mixture and roll into balls. Dust in cinnamon and xylitol if wished.

Store in the fridge for 1 week.

MAKES 20

100g pecan nuts, lightly toasted

1 tbsp ground flaxseed

1 tbsp ground chia seeds

60g canned pumpkin

1 tbsp finely ground xylitol or erythritol

1 tbsp yacon syrup, almond milk or milk

1 tbsp lucuma powder (optional)

1 tsp maple syrup

2 tsp ground cinnamon

30g chocolate chips

Ground cinnamon and xylitol, to coat (optional)

PER BITE:

Calories 59kcal

Fat 4.5g (saturates 0.6g)

Carbohydrates 3g

Sugars 0.5g

Protein 1g

RASPBERRY LEMON CHEESECAKE BITES

MAKES 10

100g cream cheese

Zest of 1 lemon

1 tbsp xylitol or
granulated stevia,
to taste

1 tbsp freeze-dried
raspberries
(optional)

60g fresh
raspberries

60g desiccated
coconut or vanilla
or berry protein
powder

DECORATION:

30g desiccated
coconut

1 tbsp freeze-dried
berries, crushed

50g dark chocolate

PER BITE:

Calories 108kcal

Fat 8.6g (saturates
6.6g)

Carbohydrates 4.9g

Sugars 0.8g

Protein 1.9g

A wonderful alternative to an ice-cream dessert!
These creamy frozen nuggets are light and fruity
and perfect if you are craving pudding. Freeze-dried
berries provide a colourful topping to these bites.

Place the cream cheese, lemon zest, xylitol
or stevia, raspberries and coconut or protein
powder in a food processor and blend until
smooth. Spoon into a bowl and freeze for 1–2
hours until firm.

Place the coconut and crushed freeze-dried
berries on a plate. Take bite-sized pieces of
the frozen mixture and roll into balls. Roll in
the coconut mixture and place on a sheet of
greaseproof paper.

Heat the dark chocolate in a glass bowl set over
a pan of simmering water and stir until melted.
Transfer the chocolate to a squirty plastic bottle
or use a spoon and drizzle the chocolate over the
tops of the balls to decorate.

Place the bites in the freezer until required. Eat
straight from the freezer.

WHITE CHOCOLATE BERRY TRUFFLES

MAKES 14

125g white chocolate chips

1 tbsp unsalted butter, softened

1 tbsp coconut cream or double cream

1 tbsp xylitol (optional)

Few drops of berry fruit flavouring extract

40g fresh pitted cherries or other fresh berries

60g ground almonds or protein powder (vanilla or berry flavour)

Berry powder or crushed freeze-dried berries, for rolling (optional)

PER BITE:

Calories 97kcal

Fat 8g (saturates 3.7g)

Carbohydrates 4.8g

Sugars 2.7g

Protein 1.2g

Best eaten semi-frozen, you can use any fresh berries in the recipe. Fruit flavouring extracts are now widely available and really help to intensify the berry flavour. Do not use frozen berries as they are too wet. If you'd like to reduce the sugar content further, use a low-sugar white chocolate.

Place the chocolate, butter, coconut cream and xylitol, if using, in a pan, and gently melt, stirring all the time. Transfer to a blender or food processor, add the rest of the ingredients and process until smooth and creamy.

Chill the mixture for 3–4 hours or freeze for 1 hour to harden.

Take spoonfuls of the mixture and roll into balls. Dust in a little berry powder or freeze-dried berries, if wished, to serve. Store in the fridge for 1–2 weeks or freeze for up to 3 months.

PINA COLADA ICE-CREAM BITES

MAKES 24

250ml full-fat
  coconut milk

200g frozen
  pineapple pieces

1 tbsp lucuma
  powder (optional)

1 tsp maca powder
  (optional)

200g dark
  chocolate,
  chopped into
  small pieces

2 tsp coconut oil

50g desiccated
  coconut, to coat

PER BITE:

Calories 62kcal

Fat 4g (saturates
  2.9g)

Carbohydrates 5g

Sugars 1.5g

Protein 1g

This frozen vegan bite is made with blended coconut cream and pineapple. Maca is known to support our adrenal glands, boosting energy levels and resilience, while lucuma adds natural sweetness and fibre. You could turn these into ice pops by inserting cocktail sticks or lolly sticks into the centre before freezing.

Line a shallow tin or plastic container with greaseproof paper.

Place the coconut milk, frozen pineapple and powders, if using, in a blender or food processor and blend to a thick soft cream. Pour into the container and place in the freezer for 1 hour until firm but not too hard.

Melt the chocolate in a pan with the coconut oil. Place the desiccated coconut on a plate.

Remove the mixture from the freezer and slice into small squares. Dip these into the chocolate, coating all sides. Coat the squares with the coconut, then place back on the greaseproof paper. Store in the freezer for up to 3 months. Best eaten frozen.

GINGERBREAD NUGGETS

A perfect treat for the autumn months, these lightly spiced nuggets are naturally rich in protein thanks to the chickpeas – this may sound an odd addition but it creates a lovely creamy texture.

Place all the ingredients in a food processor and blend to form a chunky paste, but keep a little texture in the mixture.

Take spoonfuls of the mixture and shape into little balls. Roll in the cinnamon and stevia to coat.

Place in the fridge for 30 minutes to firm before eating. Store in the fridge for up to 1 week.

MAKES 24

400g can chickpeas, drained

30g ground flaxseed

1 tsp granulated stevia or xylitol

60g pecans

30g almond nut butter or other nut butter

1 tsp vanilla extract

½ tsp ground ginger

40g stem ginger

1 tsp ground cinnamon

Granulated stevia mixed with 1 tsp ground cinnamon, to coat

PER BITE:

Calories 53kcal

Fat 3.3g (saturates 0.3g)

Carbohydrates 3.5g

Sugars 1.3g

Protein 1.6g

INDEX OF RECIPES

ABOUT THE AUTHOR

Christine Bailey is a qualified nutritionist, chef, presenter and the author of over 13 recipe and health books. She makes regular appearances in the media, including the BBC's *The Truth About Sugar*, BBC's *The Truth About Stress* and Sky News. For more information, see christinebailey.co.uk.